MUSING My Way To Peace

To Peace

While loving an addict

Written by Holly Gorman

Letters to you…

These are letters from my heart about my loved one who has struggled with addiction and all the challenges and chaos it brings. The struggle has impacted my life in ways I find difficult to express. The written musings of my heart have helped me accept the circumstances surrounding my precious loved one and the difficulties in our relationship stemming from it. Maybe you can relate and find some comfort knowing you are not alone. I have built in space for you to muse about your own life and personal thoughts. Who knows, musing may help you too.

Sincerely,

Holly Gorman

Hollyjgorman@YAHOO.com

A huge thanks to my family, Darrell, Sarah, and Christa without them I would not be doing this.

TABLE OF CONTENTS

TALK TO YOU

I really *want* to **talk** to you

To **say** something.

<u>Do</u> something

Communicate

When I try; it fails

You are failed.

That hole; that space

That ever-empty **longing**

Deep in you; in all of us

You want me to fill; to fix

I am already there

I am you; you are me; we are we

As long as you stare into the emptiness

That's all you'll see

Emptiness

When I look at you

I see **greatness.**

Beauty; love; LIFE

It's there

It's always been there

You must uncover it

You must see it

It's not as you'd expect

It's more

So much more

Know it

Believe it

Embrace it

I love you

Write what the musing, *"Talk to You"*, has stirred in you:

_____

_____

_____

_____

_____

_____

_____

_____

_____

_____

_____

_____

_____

_____

_____

YOUR STRUGGLE

Your struggle

Is

Hard to watch

At least it is for me.

Seeing the challenges

Those hardships

Hardships

Of your own making

Consequences come

They are natural

For us all

Consequences

Hardships in many forms

I can see it happening

Inching closer

Ever closer to you

I want to protect you

Shield you

Guard you

I have tried

Taking your consequences

Bore your weight

So the lesson was missed

You didn't seem to notice

Notice the damage

Damage I felt

10

Hurt

Abandoned

Ashamed

But

I can't anymore

I've tried

And I want to

But

I cannot

The struggle

Your struggle

Is yours to bear

And is necessary

Just as a butterfly's

Struggle is needed to fly

11

If I help you

Shield you

Shield you from yourself

You will be weak

You will not gain

Strength

Understanding

Lessons

Gifts of the struggle

You could really die.

I will not

Can not

12

Should not step in between

You

My precious

And your struggle

That

That not doing

But being

Is

My

Struggle

Reflecting on the *"Your Struggle"* musing, can you relate?

_____

_____

_____

_____

_____

_____

_____

_____

_____

_____

_____

_____

_____

_____

_____

BROKEN DREAMS

I love you so much

Too much?

Maybe

I saw such greatness in you

So talented and able

You could do anything

Be anything

So

I let myself dream

As you grew

So did my

Dreams

Dreams for

You

Then you fell

Completely off the rails

I was frantic

Gathering the pieces

Trying

Desperately

To reassemble

Make sense of the puzzle

Reassemble my dream

I hadn't figured it out

This dream

About you

So misplaced

I cannot control you

Control of your life

That is for you to do

I can only live my life

Those dreams

The dreams for you

Were broken

Shattered, smashed beyond recognition

When I emerged

Emerged from that wreckage

I was able

To see

This life

My life

Is only

About

Me

Are there times your *"Broken Dreams"* hinder you?

_____

_____

_____

_____

_____

_____

_____

_____

_____

_____

_____

_____

_____

LIFE IS INCREDIBLE

Life is *incredible*

Incredible because it's messy

COMPLICATED, **dirty**

Short

Live looking at the *beauty*

The beauty found in the ugly

Ugly?

Like sickness, death, bad relationships

Brokenness

The downs can be *amazing*

Just pause

Pause in that moment

Dream a little

Look at it

I mean really look at it

See it, <u>be it</u>

You are it; yet separate from it.

There is a reason, a reason

<u>**You**</u>

Are here... in this moment

It's been arranged

Be open to it

Ask the question

Why?

"Life is Incredible", musing a little about it!

_____

_____

_____

_____

_____

_____

_____

_____

_____

_____

_____

_____

_____

_____

I DON'T WANT TO HIDE

I don't want to hide.

No longer in *fear.*

Fear of the little man who isn't here.

Looking.

Looking but not seeing

Because the ghosts are in our mind

The *shadows* of expectations

Lost

I can't look at it.

The pain is too great.

Expected to fix it; change it

22

All the while ignore it;

Stop

Stand strong.

I am me

Is that enough?

That is enough.

I feel what I *feel*

And know what I *know*

No amount of hiding

Will ever

Can ever

Change that

"I Don't Want to Hide", are you hiding?

_____

_____

_____

_____

_____

_____

_____

_____

_____

_____

_____

_____

_____

_____

_____

_____

THE SEE SAW

The see saw goes up

Then down.

Pendulums swing back

And forth.

They remind me of

You.

Everything is terrible; things can't get worse: Life is fine, I wouldn't change a thing

I think I am dying: Or maybe I'm lying

Too much to do, working too much: Completely

Over it, now I'm retired

Look at them; so, messed up: You do the same and thinks it's all fine

Stop

Take a moment...

Self-reflect

Don't look at him...

Her...

They ...

Or even them.

Slow those spinning plate,

Lay them on the ground.

Now

Just look around.

Life goes on.

Life goes on even without you

Controlling......enabling

It finds a way

A way to continue

Self-reflect

What is good for you?

What's the next right thing?

Have an opinion or....

Maybe not

No matter

Be true to yourself

Your Self

Sea saw will balance

Someday the pendulums will stop.

Do you feel like you are on "The *See Saw*"?

_____

_____

_____

_____

_____

_____

_____

_____

_____

_____

_____

_____

_____

_____

Give or Take

You have taken from me.

TAKEN

By exploiting my love

Love that I have for you.

You have stolen from me.

STOLEN

From right under my nose.

I didn't notice right away.

Because of the love I have for you.

You manipulated me.

Wove your tales

So that I would do as you bid.

I fell for the line because of the love I have

For you.

The worst part,

The saddest thing

Is

My heart completely breaks

To say

To admit

If you'd be real

Come to me honestly

Openly, truthfully

I would have willingly

Given to you

Are you in a similar *"Give or Take"* situation?

_____

_____

_____

_____

_____

_____

_____

_____

_____

_____

_____

_____

_____

ISOLATION

I feel alone

Isolated

No one to share
My feelings with
Even in a room
A room filled with people
I feel alone

Isolated

No one to share
My experiences with
Sitting right next to someone else
And yet I feel

ALONE

"*Isolation*" is hard, are you feeling isolation in your life?

_____

_____

_____

_____

_____

_____

_____

_____

_____

_____

_____

_____

_____

_____

_____

Turmoil

My mind is *SPINNING,*

Back and forth

Round and round.

One extreme thought to another.

From one end of the story to the other

And back again.

Emotions running wild.

Caught

I am totally

Caught

In the turmoil of

Attachment.

My attachment to you.

I am invested.

Emotionally, shamelessly

Attached to an outcome,

What I want

What I think is good

No, no great

For you.

I want what *I* think is good

More than

You want a *good life* for yourself.

Strangely enough,

I want a good life for **you**

More than

I want

A good life for

Myself.

"Turmoil", what do think of this word?

_____

_____

_____

_____

_____

_____

_____

_____

_____

_____

_____

_____

_____

_____

_____

Grateful

Being grateful

Thankful

Appreciative

For *all* things
In life.

All things!

The good, the bad
The awful.
Painful things.
I truly want to be

Grateful.

Filled with gratitude.

Thankful for the challenge

Of living with addiction

Consuming

The precious life of my loved one.

Is this possible?

Fighting with it.

Fighting over it.

Doesn't change it.

So

Maybe

Just maybe

Finding gratitude in it

Will change me.

Being thankful

For the opportunity

To grow

To change

To show patience.

Love

Unconditionally.

In a very conditional world.

So

Today,

40

I'll start

Start being grateful.

Start showing my gratitude.

Maybe,

Just maybe

I'll become grateful

For you

Think of things you are *"Grateful"* for…

_____

_____

_____

_____

_____

_____

_____

_____

_____

_____

_____

_____

_____

_____

_____

_____

_____

SAYING I'M SORRY

I don't always behave optimally!

No one does.

I want to just

Forget it.

Brush it under the rug.

A rug to cover it up.

Unfortunately,

That doesn't really work.

The memory lingers,

Surfaces periodically.

Rears its ugliness,

Lives in my heart,

Always.

So today

I will entertain

One simple thought.

I am sorry.

Stubbornly,

I hold the rug

Over the offense.

It is tiring

Distracting

And not really working.

I know it's there,

You know it's there.

Throw back the rug.

Let the light shine,

The light of love.

Love that scatters the shadow.

The shadow of doubt.

The shadow of fear,

Of unbelief.

To trust

To have the light shine

Over me; all over

In me; completely inside me

So let the light

Lift me.

45

As I say, I am sorry.

Sorry for my bad behavior.

Sorry for my ugliness.

My ugliness that spilled

All over you.

Accept that I have weakness,

But that I am

Growing.

Springing up like

A tree

Toward the

Light.

The light of

Love.

"Saying I'm Sorry" takes some self-reflection.

_____

_____

_____

_____

_____

_____

_____

_____

_____

_____

_____

_____

_____

_____

_____

_____

Gratitude

I truly want to live,

Live in gratitude.

To have a Spirit

That shines with thankfulness.

An eye to see

The beauty of life.

Even amidst the struggles

Of living.

The pain of relationship,

Bitterness of disappointment.

There

Inside those experiences,

All experiences

Is a gift.

The Gift!

The gift that

Only a life lived in

Appreciation and gratitude

Can find.

Today I will

Use my will,

Exercise my will

To live in gratitude.

To look for the gift.

The gift that is waiting,

Just sitting there,

A treasure especially for me.

I choose to

Believe the gift

IS

In the gratitude

What does the word *"Gratitude"* mean to you?

_____

_____

_____

_____

_____

_____

_____

_____

_____

_____

_____

_____

_____

_____

SHAME

I definitely feel shame.

Ashamed

Ashamed that I,

Your mother,

The one who loves you

Deeply,

Completely,

Eternally,

May have done something

Something neglectful,

Awful, irreversible,

That made this addiction,

This all consuming

Life destroying addiction,

52

Come into your life.

So vibrant, talented

Beautiful

Hopeful

Overflowing with possibilities.

And then addiction

Destruction, painful destruction.

Helplessness.

Guilt/ guilty.

I am making a decision

Today.

A choice.

A choice to save the one I can.

The only one I have influence over.

The one who needs me the most.

And this is me.

I am not perfect.

I was not a perfect parent.

I made mistakes,

Many mistakes.

Everyone does.

That doesn't lead to addiction.

That is yours to figure out.

Your path to walk.

I am guilty.

Guilty of being,

Human.

Muse about a time you felt *"Shame"* in your life?

_____

_____

_____

_____

_____

_____

_____

_____

_____

_____

_____

_____

_____

_____

CHOOSE

I remind myself that you,

You are grown.

An adult.

With all the faults that come along.

Remember that you get to

Choose.

Choose the way you live.

With all the consequences good and bad.

Just the same as me.

I don't live my life in a way,

The way others think I should.

But I live it in the way I choose.

Today, I choose to see you.

Really see you as the adult.

The grown person

That you are.

Relax into knowing,

That growth is happening.

Change is coming,

Not in my way...

But yours!

"Choose" today the next best thing for you.

_____

_____

_____

_____

_____

_____

_____

_____

_____

_____

_____

_____

_____

_____

ARRESTED

I was shocked

At your behavior.

So scared for your future.

When you were arrested,

Handcuffed,

Photographed.

What were you thinking?

Why didn't you care?

I was in fear.

A fear you didn't seem to share.

59

Quickly back at it.

Arrested once more.

Arrested again and again.

I guess this you don't mind.

Three hots and a cot,

Better than not?

Muse about a loved one being *"Arrested"*.

_____

_____

_____

_____

_____

_____

_____

_____

_____

_____

_____

_____

_____

_____

I'm Okay

How are you today?

I'm okay.

I am okay,

Okay.

Code word

For

Traumatized

Hiding

Pretending

All is well

Don't look too closely

You will see pain

Pain

From a broken heart

A heart broken

From

Loving

Deeply loving

Mournfully loving

Someone

Who

Is

An addict

Muse about those things spark you saying, *"I'm Okay"*.

_____

_____

_____

_____

_____

_____

_____

_____

_____

_____

_____

_____

_____

_____

GOLDILOCKS

Driving impaired

Is a common occurrence

The snow was deep and all over the road

You shouldn't have driven and shouldn't have drove

Thank God

When you swerved

You got stuck off the road

I'm sure it was a sight

A sight to behold

You walked in the dark

In the middle of the night

Freezing your butt off

You must have been a fright

Knocking on doors

Attempting to get in

Breaking their window

Without a second thought

Shelter and warmth

Was all that you sought

As you snuggled on the couch

You fell asleep for the night

A family arrived home

To find you there

Fast asleep and

Without a care

It's staggering
To me
The crazy stuff
That you do

Goldilocks in real life
Sleeping on the couch
I can't even imagine

Are any *"Goldilocks"* in your life or any other fable?

_____

_____

_____

_____

_____

_____

_____

_____

_____

_____

_____

_____

_____

_____

_____

CHANGED MY NUMBER

Addiction

Single minded

At least it seems so.

Calling and calling

This crisis

That crisis

Always about **you**

I don't respond

Not in agreement

Bullying begins

Berating

Belittling

Undermining as well

Why are we fighting?

I'm not even

Sure

Texting and texting

Your drug fueled

RAGE

Comes through quite clear

It's a painful decision

Because you are

So dear

I choose to save

Me

From the battle that rages

On slot of an enemy

That only you can engage

I have changed my number

I no longer care

To be a part

Of you

Trapped in despair

The snare of despair

That is drugging

And partying

I "Changed My Number", it is an option for us all.

_____

_____

_____

_____

_____

_____

_____

_____

_____

_____

_____

_____

_____

_____

PLEASE DOCTOR PLEASE

Please doctor please

I know you can't talk

At least not to me

I understand totally it's perfectly clear

But I can say what I want

And I want to be clear

I know my precious is your patient

Know she's loved much and held so dear

Know that the medicine

A medicine you prescribed

She's crushing it and snorting it

In order to get **high**

Please know I've seen this

With my very own eyes

She'll try you

Manipulate you and downright lie

Be aware what she's doing

Cannot be advised

Not by a doctor

Unless you want her to die

Please doctor please

I know you won't speak

But the law has a flaw

I need you to hear!

74

"Please Doctor Please", have you begged before?

_____

_____

_____

_____

_____

_____

_____

_____

_____

_____

_____

_____

_____

_____

SO MUCH MORE

You are so much more than you think you are

The twinkling of the Devine dances within you

You are crafted from the dust of a star

Amazingly beautiful in all you do

You are so much more than you think you are

The miracles of the universe pulse through your
veins

Let yourself bloom

From deep within where your vastness remains

You are so much more than you think you are

Remember the Grand Plan is woven deep in the fiber
of your being

There in lay the mysteries of the universe

Always there even without seeing

You are so much more than you think you are

When things happen in this life, flow with the tides
of circumstance

Restful buoyancy acceptance will give

Blessings and beauty appear if given a chance

You are so much more than you think you are

You are exactly where you should be

Confidently filled completely in trust

You need only be you joyously filled with glee

You are so much more than you think you are

Know you always existed even outside of your body

Enjoy your life it is a gift from God

This may sound incredibly strange and very very odd

You are so much more than you think you are

It may be time to start seeking

What is the purpose of this life?

It's a question we all have, honestly speaking

Everyone is so much more than they think they are

We are all incredibly created and completely
amazing

In the image of God, molded in love

But it's all covered in this Earthly hazing

Just toy with the possibility that you are *"So Much More."*

_____

_____

_____

_____

_____

_____

_____

_____

_____

_____

_____

_____

_____

_____

BIRTHDAY WISHES

Light the candles

Think of what my heart

Truly desires

Think

Of the very best things

Then

And only then

Blow out the candles

All in one huge

Breathe

The breath that expels all the goodness

Out into the world

But

And this is a big but

Never

And I mean never

Tell anyone what my wish is

Never tell my truest hearts desire

Or

It

If spoken out loud

If I give it words

Will never

Ever come true

That sounds

When I say it out loud

It sounds

Completely

Totally and assuredly

Crazy

If I never even utter

The words of my hearts

Truest desire

Of course

Without a doubt

It will never come

True

So

Starting today

I will give voice

To my hearts

Desire

I will voice

Those things

Things I hold most dear

Speak them out

With clarity

And with strength

Out into the world

Into the vastness of the universe

Come what may

I will speak!

Muse about your *"Birthday Wishes"*.

_____

_____

_____

_____

_____

_____

_____

_____

_____

_____

_____

_____

_____

_____

_____

LOOKING FOR THE QUESTION

Years ago

I drove by a billboard

You know those huge roadside signs

And

What it said

Has stuck with me

All these years

It simply said

Jesus is the answer

At the time

And for many

Many years

I wondered

About that sign

So, if Jesus is

The answer

What

Just

What is the

Question

Some years later

Still pondering that sign

I think

If I live

My precious earthly life

Like Jesus

In love

In wisdom

In peaceful contemplation

Yet willing to shake the

Dust off my feet

And walk

Just walk away

From those who

Don't want

That wisdom

I will have the

Answer

To the question

I have spent most of my life

Looking for

Keep "Looking for the Question".

_____

_____

_____

_____

_____

_____

_____

_____

_____

_____

_____

_____

_____

_____

_____

_____

WHY

I would like

Like to know why?

Why it is

You

Do what you do?

My mind

Seeks, imagines,

Thinks through

All the reasons

Reasons I can

Think of.

And

I still don't know

Why?

You do what you do?

You place yourself

Willingly

In danger

You use drugs

Drugs of all kinds

Willingly

You were kidnapped

Tied to a chair

Held at gunpoint

And yet you returned

Went back

Willingly

90

You get arrested

Handcuffed

Jailed

Repeatedly

Yet you continue to

Do illegal activity

Willingly

Why?

I want to make

Sense

Out of nonsense

And

At the end of the day

I guess

It doesn't matter

It's your life

To do with

As you please

I need to let go

Let go

Of seeking to understand

I need to let go

Let go

Of you

Ponder all the questions especially *"Why"* and muse.

_____

_____

_____

_____

_____

_____

_____

_____

_____

_____

_____

_____

_____

_____

_____

ACCEPTANCE

What is acceptance?

Accept ance

Acknowledging

Agreeing to

Is it actually liking it?

I struggle with acceptance

Accepting circumstances

So many circumstances

Of my life

Struggling against

Against those circumstances

That has only created

Sore spots

Abrasions

Wounds of all kinds

Painful and reactive spots

Maybe

Just maybe

If I come to terms

Terms of these circumstances

Acceptance

I would begin to

Heal

So today

In this moment

I accept my circumstances

I accept these things

All the circumstances

The good

Bad

And the critically painful

Embrace them

As my soulful purpose

What does *"Acceptance"* mean to you?

_____

_____

_____

_____

_____

_____

_____

_____

_____

_____

_____

_____

_____

LIFE EXPERIENCE

I have held a deep desire

A desire

To

Share with you

My life experiences

Experiences that

Are not always

Good

My urge is to protect you

Have you learn

From me

Learn from my mistakes and bad choices

But

There is always a *but* isn't there

Life does NOT

Work this way

There is no transferring

My life lessons to you

You must go

Live, love

Run, dance

And even fall

Make your mistakes

Make your own bad decisions

Those are the lessons

That are for you

Therefore, I must

Treasure my own lessons

These are precious

Gifts from

God, the Universe

The only lesson I can give

To you

Is to embrace

Embrace completely whatever

Life brings

It is all

Goodness

And just for

You

Muse about your *"Life Experience"*.

_____

_____

_____

_____

_____

_____

_____

_____

_____

_____

_____

_____

_____

YOUR WALK

I want to lead the way
Give you advice
Tell you what to do
But it never works out

You do your own thing
It hurts me to see
Your walk is so different
Completely foreign to me

Mind my own business
Stop giving advice
You know what to do
Even if it doesn't look nice

You are living your life

I only watch it unfold

Your walk is just that

And remains to be told

"Your Walk" is important too, muse about it.

_____

_____

_____

_____

_____

_____

_____

_____

_____

_____

_____

_____

_____

_____

SEEKING

I find myself grateful

For the challenges

Challenges that loving an addict has brought

In the pain

A pain like no other

I began to seek relief

Relief from that pain

The seeking has led me to finding

A journey has been taking place

Looking back over the years

Many years

I was seeking just to survive

Then my seeking turned inward

A quest to not just survive

But to live.

Live in peace

Harmony and joyousness

Not fully realized

I continue my seeking as pain points arise

Obstacles come up, some more difficult

Than others

The precious gems I uncover

Apply to my life

Even those area unrelated to addictive life

I will keep going and being aware

Along the way

Taking time to be grateful

Really seeing and seeking each day.

What are you *"Seeking"*?

_____

_____

_____

_____

_____

_____

_____

_____

_____

_____

_____

_____

_____

_____

TEARS

I have cried

And cried

Maybe one thousand

Tears

Then ten thousand

More

Did I cry

Those tears,

Were those many tears

That I shed

For you?

Or for

Me?

Was I crying out,

Out of frustration

That you

Did not do

As I think

You should

Do?

My tears flowed

They flooded out of

Uncertainty

It was all I

Could do.

So unsure of

What would,

Could,

Or maybe even

Should

Happen to you.

I have cried

Myself dry.

I have

Exhausted

The supply.

Maybe

Just maybe

I finally

Realize

The tears don't wash away

My fears

They change

Nothing

You are grown

And in charge

Of your life.

My tears

Make no difference

Embrace it

It's true

Muse about your *"Tears"* in life.

_____

_____

_____

_____

_____

_____

_____

_____

_____

_____

_____

_____

_____

_____

EGGSHELLS

Eggshells protect

Guard the goodness

The precious yolk inside.

The only way to access

To get at that

Tasty yolk

Is to

Crack that shell.

This concept

The eggshell concept

Is similar,

So much like...

Life.

Being **broken**

Being *hurt*

Emotionally

Reaping consequences

Those things that

Happen

Born out of bad

Sometimes heartbreaking choices

Is like

The cracking

Of that shell.

The shell outside

That is protecting,

Covering

The precious

Tender goodness laying

Softly

Hidden

Tenderly awaiting inside.

What is hidden behind your "Eggshells"?

_____

_____

_____

_____

_____

_____

_____

_____

_____

_____

_____

_____

_____

_____

_____

JUST WITNESS

Watching you destroy your life

Has nearly destroyed me.

I must not watch

Anymore.

Just witness.

There is a great difference

A pronounced contrast

Between

Watch and witness.

When I watch you

Living your life

Using drugs, committing crimes,

Being homeless, getting into bad

Relationships, and on and on

I find myself waiting expectantly,

Waiting with anticipation

Looking closely

For positive change

Change I have determined

You should make.

Expectation is my high.

I must stop watching

And start witnessing.

Witnessing you destroy your life

Will not destroy me.

I must only

Be a witness.

Just witness.

Someone who sees

What is happening

But stays neutral.

I will not align with

Nor support

Not favor

Any way you choose to live

Your life.

Your life

Is yours to live as you see fit.

By me staying neutral

I will not get stirred up.

I will be still.

I will still be

But only as a witness.

I will begin

To live.

Live my life.

That is how

It should

Be.

I will

Just witness.

If you *"Just Witness"*, what would your life be like?

_____

_____

_____

_____

_____

_____

_____

_____

_____

_____

_____

_____

_____

_____

_____

BOUNDARIES

Boundaries

What are boundaries?

A border or a limit

That is the definition.

I have struggled

Struggled setting a boundary

Especially when

The boundary is set

To limit you.

I feel your limitlessness,

Your incredible potential.

You are completely

And totally

Capable.

So

Why do I struggle,

To set a limit

When you are

Exhibiting destructive behaviors

Not only to yourself

But to me

As well?

Maybe

Just maybe

That says more about me

That you.

I must self-reflect.

I must dig deep.

I must meditate.

I must seek.

Seek until.

Until I find.

Find the strength,

Wisdom and understanding

To hold that boundary

That limit, the border

That keeps you

From violating

Running over

Completely shattering

Me

What are your personal "Boundaries"?

_____

_____

_____

_____

_____

_____

_____

_____

_____

_____

_____

_____

_____

_____

LISTENING

I've been told,

Instructed to

Listen to you.

Understand

I have been

Listening,

Hearing every word

You say,

To the best I am able.

I have made the

Effort.

I have struggled

To really hear

What it is you are saying.

Truth cannot be

Conveyed within words.

Words are not strong

Enough to carry

The full weight of Truth.

So, I can listen.

I have been

Listening.

But truly

Only you

Your Self

Can know the Truth

Of what you really

Are saying.

I empathize with you

But I cannot

Act on your life by listening.

I cannot carry any

Of the burden that

Is heard by listening.

I can be responsible,

Accountable

To my life's Truth.

And you

My sweet,

Rest assured,

I listened

I listen

And plan to keep listening.

But you are

Responsible to listen

And carefully consider

What you are saying

To your

Self.

What do you hear when you *listen* to your Self?

_____

_____

_____

_____

_____

_____

_____

_____

_____

_____

_____

_____

_____

_____

DON'T JUDGE ME

Don't sit in judgement

Judging my decisions

Decisions born from

Experience

My experience

Navigating challenges

Within a relationship

Of addiction

Manipulation

And, yes, lies.

Don't judge me!

When I am doing my best

In a terrible

And tragic

Situation.

I will not ever

Completely

And totally

Disown my daughter

Not ever!

Will I set boundaries?

Place limits on interactions?

Shut off financing?

YES!

I will always

Feel she can do better

But I cannot control her

This is her life to traverse.

Don't judge me!

And say hurtful things

To undermine my confidence

In myself.

I need those around me

Who will gird up my

Belief

My total trust in

What I know is right.

Maybe not right

To you or for you

But it's my life.

And I'm doing

The best I

Can do.

Don't judge me!

Encourage me

Care about me

See me as capable.

And maybe

Someday

I will

Be.

Have you ever felt like saying *"Don't Judge Me"*?

_____

_____

_____

_____

_____

_____

_____

_____

_____

_____

_____

_____

_____

_____

_____

_____

SISTER

I know I neglected you.

Neglected your needs.

You were put on the back burner.

This was done.

I am responsible.

Not because I wanted to

But out of ignorance.

You were so reliable,

Capable,

Strong.

I know you could do it.

So, my energies were directed to your sister, the squeaky wheel.

I tried,

The best way

I knew how,

To save her from herself.

Looking back,

Knowing now,

I would do life

My life

Differently.

I would pour my energies

My life forces

Into good things!

Into you!

And let the not so good,

Those things that are

Life draining,

I would let

Them dry up and blow away

Away from

Me.

I don't get a redo,

None of us do.

But I can start

Embracing goodness

Today,

This day forward.

I love you,

And I see your

Goodness.

Forgive me

My ignorance

And I thank you

For you

Precious patience!

You are truly held

In the lap of

The Divine!

Do you have someone who you neglected while dealing with someone else's addiction? If so, what would you say if given the opportunity?

_____

_____

_____

_____

_____

_____

_____

_____

_____

_____

_____

_____

_____

I DON'T UNDERSTAND

I don't understand

Why?

Why people do the things they do?

Why do they date the people they date?

Why do they say the things they say?

Why aren't they curious about the world?

Why are they not doing what I would do?

I don't understand

Why?

Why can't they see their own potential?

Why can't they see their own greatness?

Why can't they feel the stirring of God?

Why can't they wonder at what's around the corner?

Why can't they see what I see looking at them?

I don't understand

Why?

Why can't I get that it's their journey to travel?

Why can't I accept that not everyone is the same?

Why won't I mind my own business?

Why can't I live my own life without an opinion for others?

Why can't I see I can just be me?

I don't understand

Why?

What do you ask "WHY?" about?

_____

_____

_____

_____

_____

_____

_____

_____

_____

_____

_____

_____

_____

_____

I WISH I WAS PRETTY

"I wish I was pretty"

Is what you wrote

You are so young

The rules are so simple

Wash your hair

Brush your teeth

Bathe your body

Pluck, shave and scrub

All those crazy areas of skin

Love yourself with hygiene

Love yourself with patience

Love yourself until you

Have the most attractive thing

Confidence

Then self-care as a routine

It sounds simple

It is simple

But doing it takes work

Dedication, devotion

To yourself

You are worth it

Look yourself in the eyes

And know you are

Pretty!

Does anyone you know wish they were pretty?

_____

_____

_____

_____

_____

_____

_____

_____

_____

_____

_____

_____

_____

_____

PLAY THE GAME

Maybe life is really just a game.

A game to play for fun.

A game to enjoy.

Maybe?

So today, I will play the game of life.

I will play it deliberately.

When something challenging,

Difficult, tragic, sad or

In anyway uncomfortable happens

I will play my mantra card.

"This is going to be amazing for me!"

As if I received a huge gift,

A giant box wrapped in beautiful paper

Topped with a stunning bow.

On the inside there is an equally

Huge pile of poop.

I will play life' s game,

Deliberately,

And begin to look for the "pony" .

I will deliberately step into

Life' s shadow of despair

To find the secret treasure,

To touch and embrace

The beauty hidden there.

Try to have fun in your life today! What will you do?

_____

_____

_____

_____

_____

_____

_____

_____

_____

_____

_____

_____

_____

IT'S NOT TOO LATE

I know it feels like it's too late,

Like

I've missed the boat.

I'm on the wrong path,

Took a wrong turn

Or two...

I feel like I'm now too old!

I've wasted my years.

Washed in so many tears,

Trying to figure life out.

But that's not true,

Not true at all.

It's definitely not too late.

It's never too late,

To open my eyes and see.

See the beauty

That has been there

Every step of the way.

It's not too late

To be in this moment,

To live it to the fullest.

To be thankful

For it's not too late

To recognize:

I am in the exact spot

The exact place in time

That I am supposed to be!

Have you ever felt it was "too late" for you? Write it down and then look for a positive in it.

_____

_____

_____

_____

_____

_____

_____

_____

_____

_____

_____

_____

_____

_____

NO REGRETS

I've made mistakes.

Many mistakes.

I can no longer chew on them,

Regret them,

Wish them away.

I need to recognize,

Everyone makes mistakes.

Little mistakes; big mistakes,

Life changing mistakes.

It's woven into the fabric

Of living.

It's the tragedy and the joy

Of life.

It's the turning mistakes into gifts,

Through joy

The joy of living.

Looking back, reliving and regretting

Weighs heavy,

Heavy on the heart

And mind.

It becomes too much to bear.

It covers the joy that lives in this

Moment.

Learning from mistakes

Incorporating the lesson learned.

Then laugh.

Find the humor and joy

Look ever forward,

With much joy

And no regrets!

Write a regret that you have, maybe a real struggle with something in the past. Then recognize there in lays something good and beautiful. Reflect only on that:

_____

_____

_____

_____

_____

_____

_____

_____

_____

_____

_____

_____

_____

I CAN'T CARRY YOUR BAGS

I understand; your baggage is heavy.

I understand; you want me to help carry them.

I understand; the more I try to carry your burdens,

The more burdens you gather.

Neither of our burdens lessen.

I have my own baggage to carry.

I understand; to make burdens lighter they must be
unpacked.

I understand; I cannot unpack your baggage.

I understand; I can only unpack my own.

The more I work on unpacking my stuff,

The lighter the weight of my burden.

The same is true for you.

STOP avoiding your burdens.

Embrace them.

Then begin to unpack.

It will get lighter.

Have you tried to "help" someone with their burdens and you're working harder than they are? Reflect:

_____

_____

_____

_____

_____

_____

_____

_____

_____

_____

_____

_____

_____

_____

MY PAIN

Addiction is so painful to watch.

My heart aches,

Broken with grief.

The pain of our relationship has driven me to

Seek relief.

Relief from the constant ache!

This total yearning, all-encompassing pain.

Instead of giving into the pain

Seeking temporary relief,

By giving into your

Poor planning, blaming, manipulating,

Shaming

Crisis after crisis

Until I collapse from complete and total exhaustion.

I will use my pain to motivate MY change.

I will hold my boundaries.

I will do what I think is right.

I will take care of me,

By using the pain I feel.

The pain from caring about your life

More than you do.

I will care enough not to care.

Care enough about my life

To trust my Higher Power.

To trust your Higher Power to help you care

About your life.

This will free us both.

Me to be me.

You to find you.

As intended by

Nature and God.

I will use my pain

To motivate this

Change

In

Me.

"My Pain", talk about your pain and how to begin to use that pain to motivate the change you want.

_____

_____

_____

_____

_____

_____

_____

_____

_____

_____

_____

_____

_____

_____

Made in the USA
Columbia, SC
01 March 2025

54550028R00089